The Secret of Real Estate Revealed

THE SECRET OF
REAL ESTATE REVEALED

———◆———

LANCE W. DORÉ FRICS MAI

iUniverse, Inc.
Bloomington

The Secret of Real Estate Revealed

iUniverse books may be ordered through booksellers or by contacting:

iUniverse
1663 Liberty Drive
Bloomington, IN 47403
www.iuniverse.com
1-800-Authors (1-800-288-4677)

Because of the dynamic nature of the Internet, any web addresses or links contained in this book may have changed since publication and may no longer be valid. The views expressed in this work are solely those of the author and do not necessarily reflect the views of the publisher, and the publisher hereby disclaims any responsibility for them.

ISBN: 978-1-4502-7441-8 (sc)
ISBN: 978-1-4502-7442-5 (hc)
ISBN: 978-1-4502-7443-2 (e)

Printed in the United States of America

iUniverse rev. date: 06/02/2011

Contents

PART ONE

Introduction:
What Is the Big Deal?

There are 75,000,000 homeowners in the United States, and based on the average home value of $270,000, the combined total homeownership value is $20.25 trillion. Now, let's add the value of all commercial real estate. It is estimated that commercial real estate—which includes apartments, retail stores, industrial buildings, office projects, as well as a variety of special purpose properties, including hotels, senior housing, self-storage facilities, private education facilities, religious institutions, gas stations, and a variety of related medical and scientific facilities—are worth between $10.00 and $11.00 trillion combined.

We still have not accounted for the value of government property. It is estimated that the federal government owns 650,000,000 acres of land. This includes military bases, testing grounds, national parks, Indian reservations, or land leased to private commercial ventures for forestry, mining, and agriculture. Cumulatively, the U.S. federal government owns and controls 30 percent of the entire available lands in the United States. At $5,000 per acre, taking into account the contributory value of improvements, the value of government-owned land would be $3.25 trillion. This does not include the public ownership within the 50 states, 3,141 counties, and 30,000 cities. All totaled, the value of real estate in the United States conservatively ranges from $30 to $35 trillion on any given day.

Let us compare this to the New York Stock Exchange, which has a domestic market capitalization ranging from $15 to $18 trillion. So what is the big deal? The big deal is that the total value of real estate is about $15 trillion more than the total value in the stock market creating the largest single source of wealth for individuals, corporations, and municipalities. Let's face it—real estate is a big deal!

As of January 2010, the federal government's budget deficit was approximately $1.35 trillion. If the federal government consolidated and sold just 30 percent of its real estate inventory, the deficit would be balanced. Yes, real estate is a big deal.

Figures for the global markets are less defined, but the value of institutional-grade commercial real estate (excluding the United States) totals approximately $15 to $16 trillion. The top ten international commercial real estate markets are:

- Japan - valued at $2 to $3 trillion

- Germany - valued at $1.5 to $2 trillion

- United Kingdom - valued at $1 to $1.5 trillion

- France - valued at $1 to $1.2 trillion

- China - valued at $1 to $1.1 trillion

- Italy - valued at $950 to $975 billion

- Spain - valued at $600 to $650 billion

- Canada - valued at $590 to $610 billion

- Brazil - valued at $450 to $475 billion

- Australia - valued at $425 to $450 billion

Real estate has the ability to create and sustain wealth, as well as collateralize economies. Because of its significant role in private investment and public position, it is highly beneficial to understand the fundamentals of real estate. This understanding will reveal several secrets that will minimize the risk of any real estate investment.

The Big Crash

While real estate can provide significant wealth and stability, it is subject to predictable cycles. Real estate is dynamic—there will be periods of appreciation, stability, depreciation, and revitalization. This book will help to understand this predictable cycle.

Let's look at what happened during the most recent real estate crash between late 2007 and 2011. Depreciation of home values ranged from 10 to 40 percent, depending on location and specific property type. Commercial values declined from 20 to 60 percent. I will reveal the predictability of these declines in Chapter 4, but simply put, there was both too much money and too little money.

"Easy money"—or the significant availability of borrowed funds—was created by loose fiscal policy. This ease of money allowed both under- and unqualified individuals and corporations to borrow on time. Time was created by adjustable loans with beginning teaser rates—but, the piper must always be paid.

Irrational exuberance blinds people to real estate fundamentals. For example, as the costs of borrowing increased, the flip side of the coin came up tails—and, now there was no money, or not enough money, to repay the lender. Why? Because the unemployment rate increased due to economic and governmental shifts in policy. Thus, the unraveling and downward spiral of real estate values began.

Real estate cycles are inevitable, but if you are knowledgeable about the fundamentals, you can maximize the return on your real estate investments, whether you purchase a home, apartment complex, office high-rise, industrial distribution facility, or retail corner store. The fundamental criteria that the most sophisticated real estate investors utilize in making investment decisions can be simplified into basic real estate truisms. However, first the basics need to be established in order to create common ground and benchmarks. On the following pages, I will introduce the players, the geography of the playing field, and the methodology of analyzing data.

Chapter 1—The Players

Buyers and Sellers

A market cannot be created—and value cannot be sustained—without the interaction of buyers and sellers. This is self-evident, but often overlooked, in the context of supply and demand. Too many buyers of real estate increase demand and reduce supply resulting in an increase in values. The opposite—too many sellers of real estate—decreases demand and increases supply resulting in a decrease in values.

Throughout 2009, there was a stalemate resulting from the Ask and Bid Relationship—the amount by which the ask price exceeds the bid. This is essentially the difference in price between the highest price that a buyer is willing to pay for an asset and the lowest price that a seller is willing to sell it. Beginning in 2009, and continuing into 2010, most major real estate assets had asking prices that were typically based on the sellers' perception of price levels from six to twelve months in the past. At the same time, buyers' bid prices were typically based on the anticipation of values six to twelve months into the future. This created a twelve to twenty-four month value perception gap. Transaction levels from nearly all U.S. brokerage firms were down 70 to 80 percent from 2006 and 2007 levels because of this chasm that could not be bridged.

A buyer is motivated to purchase for a variety of reasons, including diversification of portfolio, return on investment, risk mitigation, pride of ownership, and altruism. Not all real estate is purchased solely for profit, but often for intrinsic and emotional value as well.

With some exceptions, a seller is motivated to dispose of real estate for similar reasons, including consolidation of portfolio, return of investment, risk mitigation, or a forced sale due to bankruptcy or contractual obligation.

Understanding the mindset of buyers and sellers, and the motivation of each player, is fundamental to understanding your real estate.

Lenders and Borrowers

If buyers and sellers symbolize the foundation of the home, lenders and borrowers symbolize the walls, plumbing, electrical, and roof. Borrowers are included in this relationship because not all buyers are borrowers. Those buyers in possession of ample cash do not require the assistance of lenders to build their home from start to finish. However, more than 80 percent of all real estate transactions involve money borrowed from a lender. The lender can be your uncle, aunt, or a federally regulated institution, such as a bank, credit union, or insurance company.

A lender can provide money in two ways: 1) a debt instrument that requires you to repay the loan based on specified terms, or 2) equity participation. A debt instrument is a loan that includes terms such as a loan amount, interest rate, and amortization period. The payback structure can have many variations, such as full amortization, a balloon payment, and/or an adjustable interest rate. Equity participation provides funding through an investment partnership. The equity partner will not require loan payments, but rather a "piece of the action" from any net income generated by the property or realized appreciation once the asset is sold. Typically, the anticipation is for a return greater than that obtained through a standard loan. This brings to light a truism in real estate that should never be dismissed—the greater the risk, the higher the expected rate of return and, conversely, the lower the perceived risk, the lower the rate of return.

Borrowers are a fickle bunch and may have very different motivations. They generally fall into the following categories:

Owner/borrower—An owner/borrower seeks to own and use the real estate for his personal benefit, which is usually a combination of "pride of ownership" and a business venture. This type of borrower is the most secure from a lender's point of view. When Bank of America was established in 1910, this type of borrower was the cornerstone of their lending platform. The owner/borrower typically wants to purchase a home or grow their business using long-term loans with stable amortization periods and low payments obtained from a lender with whom they have an ongoing relationship. The lender is usually motivated to offer favorable loan criteria because their risk position is perceived to be minimized.

Investor/borrower—The investor/borrower is nearly the opposite of the owner/borrower. Their real estate is typically an impersonal addition to their investment portfolio, or a "means to an end." The endgame is profit and return and "pride of ownership" is secondary. If capital improvements or significant retrofits are required, they are usually the result of a comprehensive analysis of return on investment and/or motivation to remain competitive in the marketplace. The reason fast-food restaurants often undergo remodeling even if the improvements are still both physically and economically sound is to stay abreast of the market and customer demands. The investor/borrower typically wants short- to mid-term loans and will request or accept irregular amortization periods (e.g., balloon loans), modest down payments, adjustable interest rates, and a business relationship with the lender. The lender may or may not be motivated to offer competitive loan criteria based on a thorough assessment of their risk position by the loan committee. In the vetting process, many factors are considered including, but not limited to, the credit worthiness of the investor/borrower, the history of experience with previous management, investment in similar property types, recourse or non-recourse loan terms, and the equity position (commonly referred to as the "skin in the game").

One of the fundamental breakdowns that occurred in the recent recession was a motivation to increase short-term profits and stockholder value on the part of financial institutions. Previously sound lending practices succumbed to the following:

- Investor/borrowers being offered long-term amortization periods;

- Investor/borrowers being offered favorable interest rates or payback periods;

- Investor/borrowers being less scrutinized by loan committees in order to "retain the client";

- Investor/borrowers being allowed to have "no skin in the game," emphasizing the investor's credo—"Use other people's money."

These lending criteria are a recipe for failure. The question at hand becomes, "Who will be left holding the bag?" In this recession, every participant in the business cycle—the borrower, the lender, and the taxpayer—were left holding the bag.

Speculator/borrower—The speculator/borrower is similar to the investor/borrower, but while the investor/borrower typically has hard assets to use as collateral, the speculator/borrower has little or nothing to show to the lender. A good representation of a speculator/borrower is a developer. Examples of developer projects include:

- Proposed new construction, such as a spec home or office building;

- Proposed subdivision projects, either with or without entitlements; and

- Any type of land that is or is not intended for development.

Proposed projects represent the highest risk to the lender, and the criteria for due diligence exponentially increase. Significant resources are required to determine the level of confidence that must be met to make a sound loan. Areas of increased due diligence include:

- Market and feasibility studies analyzing supply and demand for the proposed project and addressing competition and absorption;

- Appraisals that assess all levels of risk associated with each stage of development and overall exposure to the lender. The values typically required include, but are not limited to, the "as is" value of the property, the hypothetical value assuming entitlements and/or completion of construction, and/or the hypothetical value assuming stabilized occupancy.

- **Management/developer experience evaluation—** Many speculator/borrowers come to the lender with "gifts and promises" that must be thoroughly researched to evaluate their actual reputation and level of experience.

- **Financial Analysis—**The best and worst case scenarios of the project must be thoroughly analyzed, including projections of:

    ◦ Rental income or gross sales;

    ◦ Vacancy and/or absorption;

    ◦ Expenses;

    ◦ Real estate taxes for the completed project;

º   Insurance costs;

º   Maintenance or homeowner association dues (HOA);

º   Utility costs;

º   Security or doorman/concierge services; and

º   Reserve requirements for capital projects.

The endgame for the speculator/borrower is profit, return, and pride/ego. This type of borrower can be both the most successful (determined by profit and return) or the most unsuccessful (determined by bankruptcy). The FDIC took 25 banks into receivership in 2008, 140 banks in 2009, and approximately 151 banks in 2010. About 80 percent of the loans funded by each of these failed institutions involved speculator/borrowers who were unsuccessful in realizing their dream.

The speculator/borrower typically wants any loan term or program that will allow them to succeed. While this comment is made somewhat flippantly, it is imperative to understand that this type of borrower is not necessarily concerned about the short- or even mid-term objectives, but rather that the dream is realized. The loan process is not the means to the end, but rather a necessary evil.

Landlords and Tenants

When landlords (property owners) rent to tenants, their ownership interest is known as the leased fee estate. With this type of agreement, a property owner relinquishes certain rights to their property to a tenant in exchange for monthly or annual rent.

Landlords typically manage the property in three different ways:

- A professional management firm that interacts on a day-to-day basis with the tenant may be retained. In exchange for a pre-determined fee or a percentage of the gross rent, the firm collects all rents, services the tenant(s), supervises project maintenance, and provides employee management (human resources) and financial and auditing services. A professional management company can be on- and/or offsite.

- The landlord can opt to self-manage the property. This is typically done to save costs and some landlords consider it part of their job.

- A landlord can also allow the tenant to act as the manager. This is facilitated through a triple-net lease, which is common for long-term tenants such as grocery stores, pad-site retailers (fast food), and some large corporate and industrial users.

Tenants pay rent to landlords. Their ownership interest is known as a leasehold estate. Simply put, a tenant retains the rights of ownership that are stipulated by a lease. Note that the market does not typically recognize a tenant's leasehold interest in a lease of less than twelve months duration. While a tenant has legal interest in the real estate as conveyed by a 12+ month lease, they may also have a value interest in the property. This occurs when the contract rent is lower than the current market rent. In cases of ground leases, which typically have terms of thirty years or greater, the lack of timely adjustment to market trends may create a significant value interest in the property. The terms and conditions regarding the allowed use of the property and the responsibilities of the landlord and tenant are detailed in standard lease contracts. When a lease is not in place and there is still occupancy, either hostilely or by silence, a month-to-month lease is in effect.

Governments are often overlooked or misunderstood players in the real estate market. The federal, state, county, city, township, borough, or community government entity is a public owner of real estate, as opposed to all previous private ownership examples. A public owner is subjected to a higher level of scrutiny and, conversely, retains a higher level of authority. Scrutiny comes in the form of public input and hearings, environmental mandates, legal obligations, and significant disclosure requirements. Authority of the government is primarily manifest in its ability to absorb property through the eminent domain process or to alter or create land uses through zoning regulations. Note that most U.S. military bases are exempt from land use and zoning regulations. Government participants otherwise behave and transact the same as the private players.

The Bench

While the real estate mantra to identify a quality real estate investment is "Location, location, location", the mantra for identifying a quality real estate consultant is "Experience, experience, experience."

The last real estate downturn occurred in the early 1990s, and lasted until the early 2000s. Most real estate cycles tend to go from peak to peak, or trough to trough, in ten- to twelve-year cycles. Why? First, the majority of people selectively focus on the "rags to riches" stories, with very few remembering the "riches to rags" stories. Mortgage brokers, investment brokers, consultants, and many of the decision makers in the real estate process tend to dissipate during the bad times. When downward cycles occur, employment in the ancillary service sectors diminishes. Those real estate professionals with institutional memory leave the business creating a void in experience and skill. In this intellectual vacuum, very few that remain have the experience or scope to truly understand the layers of investment criteria. Examples include the young MBA on Wall Street who made decisions, oftentimes involving billions of dollars, during the up cycle and who believed that all real estate transacted at six percent capitalization rates and rental escalation should always be projected at five percent per annum. They do not have the experience to react intelligently to the yellow or red flags of an impending downward cycle. It is crucial that all real estate participants have enough experience—both in the specific market with the particular property type and the real estate cycle in general—to allow them to mitigate losses or maximize profits. One size does not fit all.

Following are some of the key players on the bench:

Real estate brokers can represent buyers, sellers, or both. They can act as advocates in a transaction as leasing, transaction, or mortgage agents. Their compensation is usually in the form of a commission based on a percentage of the sale price, lease, or loan amount. Real estate brokers are required to be licensed and have continuing education requirements.

Real estate appraisers provide valuation services for a variety of participants in the real estate process, including lenders (equity and debt), attorneys, buyers, sellers, and title firms. They typically act as an independent (non-advocacy) party on behalf of their client. Their compensation is either a predetermined set fee or hourly rate and, by law, cannot be based on any contingencies or commissions with a few rare exceptions. Real estate appraisers are required to be licensed or certified and have continuing education requirements.

Loan officers provide mortgage approval through a committee process. They typically represent the borrower and can act as the loan representative between the borrower and the lending institution. Their compensation is usually in the form of a base salary plus commission (based on the loan amount) or commission only. Loan officers are not required to have a license and do not have continuing education requirements.

Escrow officers/agents provide processing and contractual support in the real estate process, supporting all parties including the buyer, seller, loan officers, appraisers, brokers, and consultants. They act as independent facilitators who ensure that all the contractual and loan obligations are met by all parties. Their compensation is a predetermined fixed fee or hourly rate. Escrow officer/agents are not required to have a license and do not have continuing education requirements.

Attorneys provide independent legal consultation and contractual support to all participants in the real estate including brokers, appraisers, loan officers, and escrow officers. They also have the legal authority to act as leasing, transaction, or mortgage agents. Their compensation can be a predetermined fixed fee or hourly rate or commission based. Attorneys are required to be licensed and have continuing education requirements.

Consultants encompass a wide variety of specialists that are often required based on the real estate's specific geography, construction type, or property type.

- **Land Planners**—A principal consultant for proposed or new construction is the land planner, who will incorporate the myriad of regulatory concerns pertaining to development (e.g., zoning regulations, specific and general plans, environmental impact reports, general engineering studies, etc.).

- **Engineers**—New construction projects will require the extensive use of engineers for soil, hydrology, traffic, civil (structural and infrastructural), and seismic studies.

- **Biologists/Environmental Specialists**—The services of biologists and environmental specialists are required to conform to regulations specific to protected or endangered plant and/or animal species.

- **Economists**—Economists provide advisory services, primarily to the buyer/developer, attorneys, and appraisers, specific to the financial feasibility and demand for the project. They act as an independent (non-advocate) party for the client. Their compensation is a predetermined fixed fee, hourly rate or commission. Economists are typically PhDs, or highly specialized consultants, and are not required to have licenses or certifications.

It is critical to choose the players on your "Bench" wisely. Their skills and experience are critical to mitigate the risk of a project allowing for the best possible outcome.

Chapter 2—Under It All Is Land

Mark Twain once said, "Buy land—they're not making it anymore." This simple truth is the cornerstone for investing in real estate. In this seven-word sentence, Twain conveyed the concept of supply and demand and the inherent worth of land as a resource and commodity.

Land is the foundation on which real estate improvements are constructed. The universal truism of "Location, location,

location" communicates that the fixed location of land can be either a positive or negative influence making it imperative to choose land carefully.

A single family home on a sloping parcel of land that fronts a body of water and/or has views is typically regarded positively in the market—not because of the specific improvements, but rather based upon its specific locational characteristics as they relate to a single family residence. The same home on a level parcel of land that fronts a trafficked highway, or abuts an industrial distribution warehouse, would be viewed negatively in the market—again, not due to the improvements themselves, but because these influences detract from the enjoyment of a single family residence.

Conversely, an industrial building on a sloping parcel of land that fronts a body of water and/or has views is typically regarded negatively in the market—not because of the specific improvements, but rather based upon its specific locational characteristics as they relate to an industrial property. The same industrial building on a level parcel of land that fronts a trafficked highway, or abuts a distribution warehouse, would be viewed positively in the market—again, not due to the improvements themselves, but because industrial usage requires good access to transportation corridors, a sizable usable site area, and proximity to employment centers in order to maximize the value of the land.

These two examples illustrate the tragic error that may occur if the relationship between the characteristics of the land and the improvements is not properly understood. The crucial physical characteristics of land that must be considered when planning the intended development or analyzing existing development include:

- Topography—Level sites are usually preferred for commercial or industrial projects, while sloping terrain enhances, and is typically preferred, for most residential projects.

- Access—Ingress and egress is a significant feature of commercial and industrial projects. One-way streets or limited turn lanes can significantly impact the competitive edge of a project. Ingress and egress are not as critical for single family residences. In fact, many residents prefer the added privacy achieved through limited or regulated access. Hence, the popularity of gated residential communities.

- Utilities—Electricity, gas, water, sewer, cable, and telephone are the most common public utility systems. The availability of wireless internet is also becoming a significant differentiator in the market. Commercial and industrial projects must meet the minimum market expectations for utility availability in order to be competitive. Residential requirements tend to be more liberal and vary by location. Typically, a combination of public connections and private systems is accepted. Examples of private systems include wind power or generators for electricity, propane or kerosene for gas, springs and wells for water, and septic systems for sewer.

- Environmental—Several geographic concerns include, but are not limited to, seismic and flood zones, biological influences, and view sheds. Not only does land encompass the surface area, but also what is below the surface (subsurface) and above the surface (supra-surface). These additional layers can influence a property through mineral and air rights. The ultimate impact of each of these environmental concerns on a property will vary from region to region and is largely based on how it is regulated by the local governing agency.

All of these physical features form the complete picture of land—the foundation of every real estate project.

Chapter 3—The Core Four

There are four core property types...residential (single and multi-family), commercial, industrial and retail. Specialty properties are not in the mainstream and are not commonly exchanged and are reviewed here as well.

Residential

A typical residential property consists of a single family home or a unit in a multi-family development. Units can be occupied by the owner, rented to a tenant through a month-to-month or long-term lease (usually twelve months or greater). The following are common residential property types:

- Houses
- Condominiums
- Townhouses
- Apartments

- Co-ops

Residential properties are significantly impacted by the subjective emotional appeal of factors such as architectural style, views, schools, traffic, proximity to employment, and neighborhood support (e.g., police, fire, community centers).

Office

Office properties consist of both single- and multi-use projects. They can be owned for the sole or partial use of the owner to support their business (such as doctors, engineers, architects, and other professional services) and corporations (such as Exxon, McDonalds, Microsoft, and others), or partially or completely leased to tenants. Tenancy can be month-to-month or subject to a long-term lease (usually twelve months or greater). The type of lease varies and is based on whether the owner (lessor), the tenant (lessee), or a combination of both pays the expenses. The following are common types of office properties:

- High-rise multi-tenant
- Corporate single tenant
- Mid-rise single or multi-tenant
- Medical centers
- Call centers

Key factors influencing office projects include:

- Tenant improvement or interior build-out

- Parking ratios
- Available utilities and local rates
- Core factors or common-area efficiencies
- Floor-plate efficiency
- Proximity to services

Industrial

Industrial properties consist of single- and multi-use projects. They can be owned for the sole or partial use of the owner to support their business or partially or completely leased to tenants. Tenancy can be month-to-month or subject to a long-term lease (usually twelve months or greater). The type of lease varies and is similar to office projects (based on whether the owner and/or the tenant pay the expenses). The following are common types of industrial properties:

- Manufacturing and processing facilities
- Distribution facilities
- Warehouses
- Research & development and scientific facilities
- Data centers

Key factors influencing industrial projects include:

- Access to utilities for meeting specific project demands
- Building or clear height, particularity for warehouse and distribution facilities

- Turning radius (to support truck maneuvering)
- Proximity to employment bases

Retail

Retail properties consist of single-use, free-standing, and multi-tenant projects. They can be owned for the sole or partial use of the owner to support their business (such as restaurants, drugstores, and gas stations) or partially or completely leased to one or more individual tenants. Tenancy can be month-to-month or subject to a long-term lease (usually twelve months or greater). Unlike most office and industrial leases, retail leases tend to be structured with the tenant paying all operating expenses with significant negotiations for tenant improvement allowances. The following are common types of retail properties:

- Neighborhood centers typically anchored by grocery stores with several complementary local or small chain tenants such as dry cleaners, postal services, and sundry retailers;
- Community centers typically anchored by national chains (such as computer, office-supply, furniture or clothing stores) with numerous complementary local or chain tenants;
- Regional malls typically anchored by one or more department stores with numerous specialized chain tenants; and

- Power centers typically anchored by three to five national department stores and several specialized chains with few local tenants.

Key factors influencing retail projects include:

- Access to and from streets and highways
- Exposure to customers
- Complementary distribution of retail tenants
- Proximity to a supportive population base

Specialty Properties

Specialty properties are those that are unique and have a limited market, or pool of buyers and sellers. Examples of specialty projects are:

- **Resort Properties** (such as amusement parks, sports stadiums, hotels, motels, and golf courses) are specialized recreational projects relying on destination-driven demand. Management acumen is critical to these types of projects because of the high degree of business enterprise intertwined with the real estate.

- **Subdivisions and Master Plans** include both horizontal and high-rise condominium projects. With these types of projects, income is generated exclusively from the sale of the individual units by the developer to the individual homeowners. Organizational acumen is critical to these types of projects because of the timing and coordination of a multitude of contractors, subcontractors, and consultants.

- **Public/Civic Facilities** consist of schools, hospitals, police stations, fire departments, parks, community centers, and open space corridors. These are publicly owned and managed by a local, state or federal agency. Fiscal support is critical to these projects in order to maintain both the facility and operations. Under-served civic projects have a residual impact on surrounding private property.

- **Utility Facilities** consist of specialized energy projects, substations, and distribution and transmission corridors (such as oil and gas farms, hydroelectric, natural gas, coal fire, nuclear, and geothermal, wind, solar, and biofuel alternative energy facilities). These projects can be either publicly or privately owned and are highly regulated and impacted by a myriad of political, environmental, and social considerations.

- **Senior Care Facilities** consist of specialized elder-care projects with a wide assortment of active living and medical support (such as seniors-only apartment complexes and congregate care assisted living, continuum of care, and hospice facilities. Management acumen and skilled employees are critical to these projects in order to maintain occupancy levels and overall success.

- **Agricultural, Ranch, and Conservation Lands** are also considered a specialty property. Agricultural operations include grove and row crops, which are highly dependent on soil quality and utility availability. Ranches can be a combination of animal grazing and residential and ancillary uses. Conservation land is recognized for its unique physical, plant, or animal habitats.

- **Green Buildings** are increasingly becoming a significant economic and social concern for commercial projects. The leading organization in providing the LEED certification is the U.S. Green Building Council. The certification is intended to provide building owners/operators guidelines for implementing measurable green building design, construction, and maintenance solutions. The most common green systems are water recycling, electrical consumption, heating and cooling systems, sewer treatment, and sustainable materials and serve to reduce the "carbon footprint" of a property.

Chapter 4—Creating Value

It is possible to actually create value. De Beers did exactly this with the diamond. The diamond was not a highly precious stone before they created demand through a brilliant marketing campaign and tight control of supply by monopolizing ownership. With their slogan, "A diamond is forever", De Beers created the desire for the diamond in everyone who fell in love, which is most of world's population.

The four critical ingredients that were necessary to create value in a diamond are identical for real estate. Maximum value is created when all of the following criteria are achieved:

Demand—Demand is the volume of desire of a purchaser for any given commodity. In some cases, only one person (volume of desire)—such as a collector of art—can create sufficient demand. The same is true if many people (volume of participants) want the same object. Obviously, the highest demand is achieved when there is both volume of purchasers and desire.

Usefulness—Usefulness is the ability of something to be used in a variety of ways. The greater the amount of options and level of adaptability, the more useful an object. Specific to real estate, the more property types that can be developed on a particular parcel of land, or the more allowed uses of a building, the more valuable the property. The adaptability of real estate refers to its ability to be converted from one use to another. For example, the conversion of an apartment building to condominiums or a motel, or an historical house to a professional office or museum. The greatest utility of a proposed or existing project is achieved with the highest number of alternatives. Conversely, the least utility is achieved when there are little or no available alternatives. Although rare, a property can have no usefulness—for instance, contaminated ground or hazardous improvements resulting in negative utility, or detriment, to the owner.

Scarcity—Scarcity is the perceived uniqueness and limited availability of an object. Perception ("Beauty is in the eye of the beholder") influences the market and the market dictates what is unique and important. This can be a waterfront home, a flag lot, or a LEED-rated facility. Once the market denotes uniqueness, the number of properties will determine the level of scarcity.

Money—Money creates the ability to actually purchase the property. Money is available through personal resources (such as cash in the bank or "under the mattress") or through financing (using a traditional lender or equity partner). Even if demand, usefulness, and scarcity are present at strong levels, it is all for naught if the asset cannot be purchased. The primary reason that real estate is so influenced by the fluctuation of interest rates is due to the direct impact on the ability of borrowers to receive loans in order to complete the purchase. If the availability of loans is reduced, real estate transactions decrease and the house of cards starts to fall. Therefore, the larger the pool of available funds, the higher the values; the less funds that are available, the lower the values.

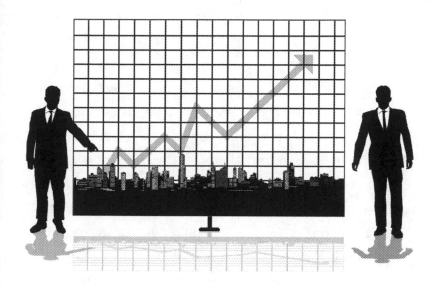

Chapter 5—Enhancing Value

There are a variety of factors that enhance the value of real estate. Here's a simple analogy—a gardener plants a seed and the seed grows into a flower. The flower needs sun, air, water, and fertile soil to enhance its continued development, growth, and longevity. If any of these ingredients are missing, the flower will likely suffer. The same is true for real estate if certain ingredients are missing. The following "ingredients" can have a significant impact on real estate:

Society—Our societal culture impacts the real estate market in both factual and perceptual ways. The most common social influences are population and demographic trends, such as age, family status, gender, and race, and crime rates.

- **Population is** a prime factor influencing real estate values. Population trends are a reliable predictor of demand levels for all types of properties. If a project adheres to market parameters and is located in an area experiencing population growth, demand will tend to increase pushing the value upward. For example, an industrial project is much more likely to thrive in an area with a large pool of skilled and/ or unskilled workers, whereas a declining population and shrinking labor pool would significantly reduce the demand for the project. The loss of the work force, and the income that once went back into the local economy, impacts retail, office, and residential development as well.

- The dominant **age** range of the population is another prime factor influencing real estate values. A younger population (from approximately eighteen to thirty-four years of age) does not typically have adequate income levels necessary for the ownership of (or investment in) real estate. However, they do support the need for rental properties. A middle-aged population (from approximately thirty-five to sixty years of age) typically does have income levels that support ownership of (and investment in) real estate. An older population (from approximately sixty-one to over eighty years of age) typically subsists on retirement and inheritance income and tends toward downsizing into condominiums and other senior-related projects (e.g., assisted living, congregate care, and medical facilities).

- **Family status, gender, and race** refer to the ratio of singles versus married people, males and females, and racial distribution. These important demographics help to assess not only overall demand, but the specific type of construction (e.g., retail, office, industrial, apartment, single family homes, etc.). For example, an area with a high percentage of large families will require single family housing with a greater number of bedrooms and more retail services.

- **Crime rates** impact the level of security and stability within an area and will influence construction and maintenance requirements. Areas with a high crime rate will often require fencing, alarm systems, and/or security guards.

Economic—The local, regional, and national economies have the ability to enhance real estate due to the direct effects on fiscal and monetary policies, as well as interest rates. This is best represented by the concept that real estate investment is premised on an underlying economic principle that there is profit to the entrepreneur, which is comprised of the remaining agents of land, labor, and capital.

- Median **income levels** influence real estate development trends and offer continued support to existing projects. Higher income levels tend to support luxury single and multi-family housing, boutique retail outlets, corporate office complexes, full-service hotels, and research and development projects. Lower income levels tend to support entry-level single family and affordable multi-family rentals, discount retail centers, incubator industrial complexes, and office and motel projects. Income levels can be dispersed across entire cities or communities or can be pocketed within specific neighborhoods. Once projects are developed, continued support will partly depend on the stability of income levels. For example, a discount mall may have to re-tenant if income levels significantly increase, thus enhancing values. Conversely, a project occupied by boutique retailers may have to re-tenant in order to compete and sustain its value if income levels significantly decrease.

- **Interest rates** determine mortgage payment amounts and have a significant impact on the value that can be achieved for any particular property. Assuming a fixed loan amount, the lower the interest rate, the lower the mortgage payment resulting in more available funds, increased demand, and enhanced values. This occurred in the mid-2000s, where low interest rates drove demand for housing and real estate. The converse is also true—increased interest rates "lock out" borrowers from qualifying due to prohibitive debt-to-income ratios and stricter loan criteria.

- **Employment rates are** one of the single best indicators of the direction of real estate trends. Historically, an unemployment rate of less than five percent has been indicative of an accelerating real estate market where competition for product increases. An unemployment rate between five and eight percent generally denotes a stable real estate market with equilibrium in supply and demand. An unemployment rate greater than eight percent is typically present in a declining real estate market where decreased income levels result in a drop in demand. The real estate cycle that occurred from 1999 to 2009, was affected by all three of these scenarios. Employment rates must be carefully analyzed as they can affect local and national economies differently. Some local economies have single-source employment (e.g., military, automotive, financial, oil, and gas) that can have a sweeping "all or nothing" effect on its real estate values. A diversified employment base tends to stabilize real estate markets.

Government—Local municipalities, state agencies, or the federal government affect real estate from a regulatory standpoint. Whether this effect is positive or negative depends upon the market's reaction to the imposed requirements. Typical governmental regulations include:

- **Zoning:** Zoning designations are the most basic regulatory vehicles for real estate. They impose a variety of conditions on a property including, but not limited to, what particular use is allowed (such as residential, multi-family, office, industrial, resort, retail, parks and community facilities, etc.) and development guidelines (such as number of floors, maximum coverage, parking requirements, landscaping requirements, etc.). Additional regulatory instruments that must be considered include:

  General plans—typically a regional plan that specifies municipal goals over a 10+ year period;

  Specific plans—typically a neighborhood plan that specifies municipal goals over a one to five year period;

  Tentative maps—approvals for an individual project that fall under the jurisdiction of a specific plan; to be completed within a one to three year period.

- **Taxes:** Municipalities tax real estate to support police, fire, safety, and general regulatory management. Tax levels are of consequence to large employers creating competition among cities to attract employers (such as Wal-Mart or Google). The market typically reacts unfavorably when tax rates change within the short term and favorably when tax rates can be predicted from one year to the next. A supplemental tax known as a "special assessment" is usually project-specific and funds such services as schools, roads, and utilities.

- **Public Services:** Public services that are managed or supported by the government include police, fire, refuse collection, and transportation. A minimum level of service is mandatory for any community and maintains the balance between supply and demand for real estate. Well developed public services almost always enhance real estate values because the perception of risk is lessened. Transportation systems are a double-edged sword that can enhance or detract from a community. For example, many cities are implementing trolley, subway, and bus systems, which expand the distribution of the population base and increase demand for real estate. However, at the same time, increased distribution of the population can lead to higher crime rates and inadvertently have the opposite (negative) effect on real estate. For this reason, exclusive neighborhoods or communities often reject increased access.

Environment—Those physical and environmental conditions, both inherent and external to the real estate, that can enhance or detract from real estate values include:

- **Location**: General location (such as state, city, or town) and specific location within the neighborhood are both relevant. The market recognizes general "trophy" locations (such as New York City, Los Angeles, London, Paris, Moscow, Los Angeles, Tokyo, and Washington DC) due to their retention of a diversity of social, governmental, and economic conditions that generally stabilize the real estate market. Specific locations that enhance value can be based on a single or several amenities. For example, twenty-four hour locales (such as Las Vegas or Paris) allow the local population and employment base greater access to all businesses and services. Specific locations (such as Frankfurt, Dallas, Denver, Taipei, Sydney, Montreal or Atlanta) that focus on merging transportation hubs, including railroad, airports, ports, or highway connections. Specific locations can also be site-oriented (e.g., corner orientation, exposure to pedestrian or highway traffic, or mountain, beach, and waterway zones.

- **Permitting**—While regulatory (governmental) at first glance, permitting reflects the myriad of conditions that must be met as a result of existing physical characteristics or the pending impacts of the physical nature of the real estate. The conditions that must be met are varied and might include:

  - Seismic retrofits and/or building standards

  - Flood zone mitigation and/or building standards

  - Historical preservation or archeological mitigation

  - Environmental impact mitigation

  - Noise abatement

  - View corridor alignments

  - Climatic building standards—e.g., insulation, utilities, and windows

The degree of influence of each of these environmental characteristics depends upon the weight placed on each condition by the local market and the direct impact on a property.

Chapter 6—The Maximization of Value (or The Highest and Best Use)

Once value has been created and enhanced, it is time to maximize value. The concepts that must be considered and analyzed in order to determine a property's highest and best use apply to all types of real estate. The four considerations are legal uses, physical attributes, fiscal position and maximum profitability.

Legally Permissible

There are a number of proposed and existing projects that are either legally underutilized or not legally allowed. A "legally nonconforming" use is one that is not allowed under the current zoning regulation or general plan designation. For example, a 100-unit apartment project that was legal at the time of construction may be subject to updated regulations that now allow only fifty units. In such a case, it is critical to ensure the existing higher density project is maintained or rebuilt in the case of a catastrophic event in order to maximize the real estate investment.

Conversely, there are times when the existing improvements do not maximize the use of the site. For example, a single family residence that is situated on an acre of land in a previously rural area would be underutilizing a site that had been rezoned to commercial. In this case, the residence no longer contributes value to the land and, assuming adequate market demand, should be demolished to allow for commercial improvements that maximize value.

With proposed projects, it is critical to balance maximum allowed density with market demand. The maximum allowed square footage on a tract of land does not always create the highest value. For example, if zoning allows a 5,000 square foot single family residence on a site, but the market only supports homes up to 4,000 square feet at a sale price of $300 per square foot, the equivalent sale price for a 5,000 square foot residence would be $250 per square foot. If building costs, which do not vary much based on size, were $200 per square foot, the following profit calculations would apply to the 5,000 square foot residence:

5,000 square feet @ $250 price per square foot   = $1,250,000

Less 5,000 square feet @ $200 cost per square foot = ($1,000,000)

Profit (20% of sale price)   = $250,000

The following profit calculations would apply to the 4,000 square foot residence:

4,000 square feet @ $300 price per square foot   = $1,200,000

Less 4,000 square feet @ $200 cost per square foot = ($800,000)

Profit (33% of sale price)   = $400,000

This scenario demonstrates the importance of analyzing the legally permissible uses that are actually supported by the market.

Physically Possible

Even if a project can be legally constructed, there must be several core physical attributes and a minimum level of infrastructure present to support it. Since existing projects are clearly physically possible, this applies only to proposed construction.

Physical attributes to consider once the legally allowed use is established are:

- Access
- Utilities
- Topography
- Environmental concerns
- Labor base
- Distribution corridors (e.g., airports, freeways, waterways)

Financially Feasible

A critical test for any proposed or existing project is whether its value exceeds the value of the underlying land. In other words, confirming whether the project is financially feasible. This can be demonstrated by including the land value in the previous analysis of the two single family residences:

The 5,000 square foot house has the following profit:

5,000 square feet @ $250 price per square foot	=	$1,250,000
Less 5,000 square feet @ $200 cost per square foot	=	($1,000,000)
Profit (20% of sale price)	=	$250,000
Less Land Cost	=	($275,000)
Net Profit (Negative)	=	($25,000)

The 4,000 square foot house has the following profit:

4,000 square feet @ $300 price per square foot	=	$1,200,000
Less 4,000 square feet @ $200 cost per square foot	=	($800,000)
Profit (33% of sale price)	=	$400,000
Less Land Cost	=	($275,000)
Net Profit (10.4% of sale price)	=	$125,000

In this analysis, it is evident that the proposed 5,000 square foot house is not financially feasible because it does not contribute to the underlying land value. In other words, there is no entrepreneurial profit. On the other hand, the 4,000 square foot house indicates a positive return to the land and entrepreneurial profit.

Maximally Profitable

The question of maximum profitability more directly addresses market demand factors (potential buyers). This concept implies that of the potential uses of a property that create a positive residual land value, one use will maximize said value. Returning to the example of the two residences and adding an additional scenario, this becomes clear:

The 5,000 square foot house has the following profit:

5,000 square feet @ $250 price per square foot	=	$1,250,000
Less 5,000 square feet @ $200 cost per square foot	=	($1,000,000)
Profit (20% of sale price)	=	$250,000
Less Land Cost	=	($275,000)
Net Profit (Negative)	=	($25,000)

The 4,000 square foot house has the following profit:

4,000 square feet @ $300 price per square foot	=	$1,200,000
Less 4,000 square feet @ $200 cost per square foot	=	($800,000)
Profit (33% of sale price)	=	$400,000
Less Land Cost	=	($275,000)
Net Profit (10.4% of sale price)	=	$125,000

A 4,500 square foot house has the following profit:

4,500 square feet @ $275 price per square foot	=	$1,237,500
Less 4,500 square feet @ $200 cost per square foot	=	($900,000)
Profit (27.3% of sale price)	=	$337,500
Less Land Cost	=	($275,000)
Net Profit (5.05% of sale price)	=	$62,500

Out of the three scenarios, the project that achieves the highest profit is the maximally profitable use of the underlying land. As seen by the previous analyses, the smallest sized house (4,000 square feet) that was legally allowed, physically possible, and financially feasible brings the greatest return to the land ($125,000, or 10.4 percent of the sale price) and should be constructed.

Chapter 7—The Secret to Real Estate

Most players in the real estate game harbor a serious misconception about real estate investment. They believe that only a single or few components are necessary to achieve a maximum return. In fact, shortcutting the process most often leads to lower profits or, in worst case scenarios, a failed investment.

As discussed in Chapter 4, the first crucial step in the process of maximizing a real estate investment is to create value through analyzing the macro elements of demand, usefulness, scarcity and money. These elements form the foundation of a successful real estate project. Without them there is minimal, and sometimes negative, value to the land. If a player does not progress to the next crucial step, their investment will likely fail.

In Chapter 5, the second step—the enhancement of the investment value—was revealed. The completion of this step takes a project to the next level (or a higher worth) through an understanding of the micro elements of societal, governmental, environmental, and economic influences. Many projects progress to this level and achieve moderate or limited success, but most go no further.

The final step—the maximization of the investment value— was covered in Chapter 6. The successful completion of this step brings the highest achievable value to the real estate investment by ensuring that the project-specific goals of legal permissibility, physical possibility, financial feasibility, and maximum profitability are met.

Maximization of the investment value is the final real estate building block. The result of this step is the highest achievable value to the real estate investment. The final pillars of legal uses, physical attributes, financial feasibility, and maximum profit are the project-specific brains of the development of a successful real estate project. Few projects progress to this level, but most that do are financially successful.

The Real Estate Investment Pyramid demonstrates the connectivity of each of these steps (or "pillars") and the necessity of each one in order to achieve maximum results with any given real estate investment.

- Demand is relative to society and financial feasibility;

- Usefulness is relative to government and legal uses;

- Scarcity is relative to environmental and physical attributes; and

- Money is relative to economic and maximum profitability.

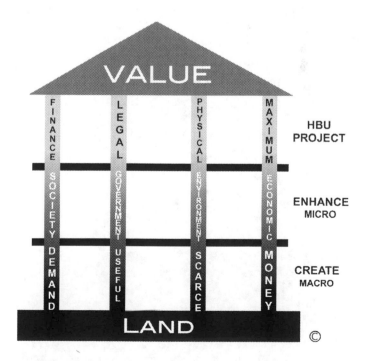

The symbiotic interconnectedness of the macro, micro and project-specific pillars, coupled with adherence to the laws of real estate, is the secret to real estate. Each component—the macro, micro, and project-specific—must combine to achieve the maximum value of a real estate investment. The macro elements (demand, usefulness, scarcity, and money) are the broadest and form the foundation of value. The next level is comprised of the micro elements (society, government, environment, and economic factors) that enhance value. The final level is project-specific (financially feasible, legally permissible, physically possible, and maximally profitable) and allows for the highest value.

PART TWO

---•◦•---

The Laws of Real Estate

There are several real estate principles, or laws, that must be understood and adhered to in order to ensure that an investment has the highest chance of success. If these laws are broken, the result will be significant deterioration, or destruction, of a successful investment. In Part 2, these laws will be presented in detail in order to increase the odds of financial success.

Chapter 8—The Law of Scales

The Law of Scales maintains that there is a need for balance in the general location of a property in regard to property types, jobs, population, community services, private enterprise, and the myriad of additional components that create a community.

There are many examples of breaking the Law of Scales, the most common being a one-industry town. This is the case with Detroit, Michigan (centered on the automotive industry), Las Vegas, Nevada (centered on gambling), and Dammam,

Saudi Arabia (centered on oil and gas). While these areas can experience extreme highs in an upward swing of an economic cycle, they tend to be devastated on the downward swing. What often results is a "domino structure". If one piece is pushed, the rest of the dominoes fall. This unbalanced structure creates higher risk as the real estate is subject to extreme fluctuations.

Larger and more diverse communities obey the Law of Scales. Prime examples of areas with a balance in social, governmental, economic, and environmental components are New York City, Paris, Sydney, Moscow, and Hong Kong,

Chapter 9—The Law of Harmony

The Law of Harmony maintains that a specific project must meet the demands of the market and it should not be expected that the market meet the demands of the project.

The best examples of breaking the Law of Harmony are overbuilt or mismatched projects. Many developers or property owners believe they know best and will maximize or exceed zoning allowances to increase development based upon their exuberant expectations of a project's profit or function. These projects get built without regard to market expectations or demand. This often occurs in retail projects near the ocean where the coverage was maximized, but pedestrian access and/or potential ocean views were blocked. I have personally inspected a residence where the owner's sense of art and architecture resulted in every room being separated by an outdoor staircase or bridge. I have seen corporate office headquarters constructed within five miles of the CEO's primary residence in a high-end suburban corridor resulting in elevated support costs due to employees traveling twenty-five to fifty miles to work. Some of the greatest real estate investment failures occur when the Law of Harmony is broken.

When the Law of Harmony is followed, projects tend to have consistently higher occupancy, rents, and absorption of units or space. These typically well-conceived projects are in alignment with market expectations of tenancy, pricing/rental levels, and architectural standards. There is a balance between project design and access to shopping, services, and community support, as well as a diversified population base minimizing risk during typical cyclical fluctuations.

Chapter 10—The Law of Limits

Simply put, the Law of Limits is knowing when to stop. Greed is typically the reason behind the violation of this particular law. Just because a 2,500 square foot house is good does not mean a 10,000 square foot house is better. Just because a 35-unit apartment project is good does not mean a 350-unit project is better. The Law of Limits addresses the concept that increasing size may increase revenue, but it can also increase construction costs and operating costs to prohibitive levels. There is a point in any project where value and profit are maximized and surpassing this point may detract from said value or profit.

Many developers of master planned communities or subdivisions break the Law of Limits when they increase the number of homes past the desired point of maximized value and profit, usually leading to increased competition and decreasing profit margins. When margins decrease, the developer is motivated to increase supply in order to maintain the level of revenues. In these cases, it is best to maintain higher margins at a level that maximizes revenues. An example of a violation of this law that made national headlines was the development of an office project near an airport. Despite FAA building height restrictions, the developer maximized the building height in order to achieve the highest rents possible. However, the building violated FAA flight pattern restrictions with the addition of the highest floor. After a lengthy court battle, the developer was required to demolish the top floor of the building at great expense.

Obeying the Law of Limits results in a balanced project that can typically sustain demand during most cycles because the project is neither over or under-built and abides by the market's expectations of quality and architecture. Similar to the Law of Harmony, these projects will typically have stable occupancy, strong rents, and exhibit overall strong demand.

Chapter 11—
The Law of Common Sense

The Law of Common Sense maintains that no one will pay more for a property than what could be paid for a reasonable substitute. This is one of the most violated laws of real estate. It is so simple to understand, but often completely ignored. The premise is to never overpay, to check your ego at the door, and understand that any property can be replaced with something else—except, of course, the Taj Mahal.

The Law of Common Sense is most often broken in for-sale scenarios where an owner or investor maintains that their property's appearance, location, quality of construction, tenant base, views, or all of the above, are ten, twenty, or even one hundred percent better than all other competing projects. In fact, there are ten, twenty, or one hundred other competitive properties that can be purchased for ten, twenty, or fifty percent less than their project. There are almost always replacements for a project, and the market is aware of them. If you see a project that has been listed for sale for more than six months in a generally healthy market, it is likely that the owner or investor is breaking the Law of Common Sense. A violation of this law results in high holding costs, extended marketing periods, and ridicule from competitors.

Obeying the Law of Common Sense usually leads to competitive projects that maximize profit because they satisfy the market's expectations of supply and demand. These projects typically sell within a reasonable marketing time and attract a volume of interested buyers allowing them to compete and maximize values. When the Law of Common Sense is followed, you will hear words such as "smart," "good deal," "lucky," or even "genius" to describe the transaction.

Chapter 12—The Law of Hope

The Law of Hope applies to both commercial and residential properties, but is most often applicable to commercial projects. This law maintains that all real estate is bought and sold with expectations—of future profit, value, or security. This hope can often blind the owner or investor, leading them into a false sense of optimism with a project suffering from deferred maintenance, poor location, or a suspect tenant mix. The reality is that most often the project will require a significant investment and may not improve at all. Even when all project-specific issues are understood and addressed, there can often be external issues (such as a bad economy or a failed local employer) that will turn the dream into a nightmare.

The violation of the Law of Hope typically stems from an owner or investor wearing "rose-tinted glasses" that obscure reality. Consequences are not immediate, but materialize six, twelve, to twenty-four months after the initial purchase or investment. The buzz words you most often hear in these situations are "It will get better," "It's only a matter of time," "We can wait this out," "This is only temporary," and/or "I have seen this before, and I know how to handle it." One example of a typical project that violates this law is a commercial property purchased at an overall or discount rate similar or lower than alternative safe rates (such as municipal bonds). Another example is a house purchased with a minimal down payment and artificially low mortgage payments (created by an adjustable interest rate) based on the expectation of future refinancing. Rampant violations of the Law of Hope was one of the primary causes of the financial crisis that began in 2007.

Obeying the Law of Hope is seen when profit expectations are supported by current rents, vacancy, and expenses, coupled with reasonable down payments and fixed interest rates. The buzz words that signify this law is being followed include "The numbers work today," "This is long-term hold," or "I can live with this." Obeying the Law of Hope is a good antidote to the inevitable fluctuations in real estate cycles.

Chapter 13—The Law of Supply and Demand

The Law of Supply and Demand is an age-old economic principle that applies whether you are selling sugar in a five-and-dime store or developing a new city in a rural area. Fundamentally, supply should not exceed current or expected demand and, ideally, they are in equilibrium. When supply and demand are out of balance, the market either under- or overreacts creating the inevitable ups and downs in the real estate cycle. This brings to the forefront another principle: real estate markets are imperfect. Market participants cannot react efficiently or effectively to mitigate an imbalance because of the nature of the supply side (because construction begins six to twenty-four months before the final product is complete). It is upon completion that a project must meet market demand. In depth market and feasibility studies can mitigate this particular risk.

Breaking the Law of Supply and Demand results in either excess profit or a lack of profit. When demand exceeds supply in a "seller's market", there is greater competition for the real estate increasing prices and returns (profit). While most people would be ecstatic with higher than typical prices and returns, this situation results in a "price bubble", inflation begins, and the bubble eventually bursts. For those few individuals who reap the excess profits during the up-cycle, that reward is great, but an individual does not create the market and the market will correct itself—usually within a short time frame.

When supply exceeds demand in a buyer's market, there is little or no competition for the real estate reducing prices and returns (profit). This can be compounded by a significant loss of jobs resulting in more significant price reductions, a decreased tax base for the local municipality, and reduced public services. This downward cycle is the sign of a recession or, when severe, a depression. Obeying the Law of Supply and Demand creates equilibrium for all property types, including housing, office, retail, industrial, and hotels. Pricing levels stabilize and tend to experience only gradual increases resulting primarily from population growth. The equilibrium in supply and demand can last from a few months to several years.

Chapter 14—The Laws of Positive and Negative

The Laws of Positive and Negative affect how a specific project relates to the market. This is yet another powerful investment strategy that is either intuitively understood or completely ignored. The Laws of Positive and Negative reflect how the value of a project is either pulled up or down by the surrounding properties.

The best example of this law is seen in the construction or remodel of a home. The Law of Positive maintains that the home should be slightly smaller in size or lower in quality than the biggest and best house in the neighborhood. Because the competitive base of the neighborhood is represented by the higher-end homes, the value of new (or remodeled) construction will be "pulled up". The Law of Negative maintains that if you build larger, or of higher quality, than everyone else in the neighborhood, you will be penalized. Because the competitive base of the neighborhood is represented by lower-end homes, the value of your new construction or remodel will be "pulled down." This is consistent with the Law of Limits, which maintains that increasing costs will not necessarily increase value or profit.

Violation of the Laws of Positive and Negative is often visual in a neighborhood or community. For example, violations are occurring in an area that is described as "eclectic" or "interesting" based on its dichotomy of project sizes, styles, and quality. There will be retail projects situated adjacent to industrial complexes or houses in an inconsistent variety of sizes and colors. It is also common to see overbuilt houses in an area predominately improved with smaller homes. Therefore, breaking the Laws of Positive and Negative most often results in an erratic pattern of development, which reduces confidence levels and stability in the market.

Obeying the Laws of Positive and Negative creates a segregation of projects based on property type, development style, or usage. While housing styles can be somewhat varied, it is within the limits supported by the local population base. Office and industrial projects meet the standards of owners, tenants, and corporations. Retails projects are occupied by a mix of local, regional, and national tenants, and the inventory of apartments meets the limits and standards set by local income levels.

Chapter 15—The Law of Phases

The Law of Phases maintains that social, economic, governmental, and environmental factors will impact real estate, creating fairly predictable fluctuations in values. Because real estate is dynamic rather than static, it is critical to know which phase of the real estate cycle you are in to maximize a real estate investment. The traditional phases are: 1) growth, 2) stabilization, 3) decline, and 4) revitalization.

The growth phase typically presents the greatest number of real estate investment opportunities. However, as more competitors enter the market, potential profits will shrink. The beginning of the growth cycle is the precise time when savvy investors will sell assets and realize maximum profits. The common stereotype that comes into play in this phase is that market participants are "aggressive, have a "herd mentality", or are "jumping on the bandwagon". I have talked with many representatives from global investment firms, REITS, and pension funds and found that while they might know it's time to leave the market, they often do not want to be the one who jumped out too early for fear that they left too much money on the table. Therefore, the "herd" continues to escalate demand in growth markets (as characterized by Alan Greenspan's label of "irrational exuberance") until the market eventually becomes rational (stabilized) or the bottom falls out (decline).

The stabilization phase is a period when cash flow from rents or sales, rather than equity appreciation, is the primary motivation for investment. Realized profit is lower than in the growth phase, which tends to attract long- rather than short-term players. Many markets can exist in the stabilization period for years at a time as long as supply and demand factors are near equilibrium and enhancements of value remain within predictable boundaries. Signs that the real estate is outside stabilized market boundaries include longer or shorter than typical marketing periods, changes in governmental mandates (e.g., zoning), dramatic increases or decreases in population, interest rate fluctuations of one percent or greater, and/or environmental factors (e.g., endangered species).

The decline phase is when real estate equity and/or income is eroded. A project can still have a positive cash flow in a declining market, but it is typically lower resulting in a reduction of equity. In a severe decline, all equity disappears and debt and expense obligations exceed net income. This is often the time when most investors attempt to sell assets, usually too late, in order to preserve what is left of their equity position. Marketing times extend significantly while the equity position continues to decrease. The common stereotype that comes into play in this market is that the investor is "left holding the bag," is "upside down," or the investment "does not pencil." Decline phases often become self-propelled as sellers dump more and more product on the market creating an oversupply that further depresses the real estate. Cash buyers will hold off on purchases as they wait for properties to be more and more distressed looking for the best deal. Downward pressure on real estate continues until buyers finally enter the market, usually with value-added plays. At this stage, the real estate is usually heavily discounted as both project and market risk have peaked.

The revitalization phase is characterized by the greatest risk due to an unstable market still in flux and, therefore, the highest profits. First time market participants may have entered the market at the wrong time or, if they entered at the right time, they may lack the management skills or expertise needed to reposition their real estate. Even if an investor timed the market right and has management expertise, they may simply run out of cash to support the real estate during this phase. However, if they can saddle the risk of the real estate during this time period, peak profits can be achieved. This is often the case in downtown urban markets where core redevelopment creates dynamic residential, retail, office, and public venue opportunities. Gentrification—where middle and upper income market participants invest in declining neighborhoods in the interest of renovation and rehabilitation—is another example. This occurred in the SOHO and East Village neighborhoods of New York City, Hayes Valley in San Francisco, and Fell's Point in Baltimore.

An investor breaks the Law of Phases when they enter or exit the market during the wrong phase. Buyers should invest in real estate during the revitalization period in order to achieve maximum profit and should buy during the growth cycle in order to achieve reasonable profits with an outlook to stabilization. Buyers violate the Law of Phases if they purchase during declining or stable markets and do not have a plan to transition to the next cycle. Sellers should divest in real estate during the growth period in order to achieve maximum profit and during the stabilization cycle in order to achieve reasonable returns. Sellers violate the Law of Phases if they divest during declining or revitalizing markets and do not have a plan to invest in real estate during the next cycle.

Obeying the Law of Phases occurs when both the real estate asset and the market participants are in unison creating an ebb and flow of investment and divestment while maintaining sustainable market equilibrium.

Chapter 16—The Law of Whole

The Law of Whole maintains that cost does not equal value. A real estate investment may be worth more or less than the actual dollars required to either purchase or build it.

Breaking the Law of Whole can be seen when an owners or builders desires or preferences are out of sync with market demand. They "know" more than the market or simply do not care about resale or investment value and construct or modify a house or project to satisfy their individual tastes. Some examples seen with homes are:

- Highly customized fixtures (e.g., lighting, windows, plumbing, cabinetry, and a variety of imported materials);
- Design mismatches where an owner wants unique architectural themes that have little or no appeal to the broader market;
- Highly customized landscape features (e.g., mature trees, water and pool features, and lighting);
- Too few or too many bedrooms and/or bathrooms for the market; and
- Conversion of garages into bonus rooms.

Some examples seen with commercial projects are:

- Excessive tenant improvement allowances in office or industrial space where retail tenant improvements are typically at the new tenant's expense;
- Inadequate or super-adequate electrical, communication, or internet capabilities;
- Reduced parking spaces (rarely are there too many spaces);
- Design mismatches where an owner wants unique architectural themes or preferences backed by little market acceptance; and
- Too few or too many amenity packages (e.g., security systems, common areas, gyms, movie rooms, and cafes.)

This law is similar to the Law of Harmony, but is more narrowly focused toward market approval of the entire project. When this law is broken, "costs exceed value." I have received actual receipts from clients itemizing their expenditures for world-class upgrades and expecting each dollar to be recouped in the overall investment value. This rarely happens. When this law is broken, the most common result is a property that remains on the market much longer than similar properties.

When the Law of Whole is obeyed, a project or house will be in alignment with market preferences. A commercial project will have an acceptable unit count, square footage, and general balance of amenities and will be neither over- or under-improved. A residence will have an acceptable size, bedroom and bathroom count and a balance of amenities. When a property matches market expectations, the common result is a typical, or slightly shorter than typical, marketing time.

In some cases, a well-conceived project will recoup every dollar spent if the market recognizes additional value above the costs. It is crucial to balance functionality and vanity. You can spend $1,000 on wood windows or $500 on plastic-clad-over-wood windows. No matter how much you spend, most double-pane windows function the same way—they keep the elements in check. To obey the Law of Whole, focus on the function of the project components and only pay for those extras that the market really desires.

Chapter 17—The Economics

There is a lot of economic modeling within the real estate market. We use terms like overall rate, capitalization rate, terminal rate, discount rate, internal rate of return, profit, net income, gross income, net income multipliers, gross income multipliers, expense ratios, vacancy rates, discounted cash flow, price per square foot, price per unit, price per room, and many others. These are all important objective calculations that help us analyze the risk position of a property and compare one real estate investment to another.

Without a comparison to the economic indicators of other real estate assets, the indicators for a single asset are irrelevant.

For example, knowing that an apartment building in midtown Manhattan has an overall (capitalization) rate of ten percent means nothing by itself. However, with the knowledge that the overall rates from twenty apartment projects in midtown Manhattan that sold in the past six months ranged from seven to nine percent, the ten percent overall rate indicates a risky project. All economic indicators must be compared to competitive rates in order to properly assess an investment's position in the market.

Here are some broad, but useful, rules of thumb derived from almost three decades of real estate investing and analysis:

- **Rule 1**—With any rates applied to any property type, the lowest rate is perceived to indicate the lowest risk and the highest rate is perceived to indicate the highest risk. With greater risk, higher returns (or profit) are expected to compensate the investor for the additional risk.

If capitalization rates for all hotel sales over the past two years in Houston, Texas, ranged from eight to eleven percent, the hotel that sold at eight percent is perceived to have the lowest risk and, therefore, the lowest return. Conversely, the hotel that sold at eleven percent is perceived to have the highest risk and, therefore, the highest return. With greater risk, represented by higher rates, greater returns or profits are expected to reward the investor as compensation for the risk.

- **Rule 2**—With any factors applied to any property type, the highest factor is perceived to indicate the lowest risk and the lowest factor is perceived to indicate the highest risk.

If an apartment project in Seattle, Washington, sold at a sixteen times annual gross income multiplier, and all apartment project sales in the past two years had factors ranging from eleven to sixteen, it is perceived to have the lowest risk and, therefore, the lowest return. Conversely, an apartment project that sold at a factor of eleven times gross is perceived to have the highest risk and, therefore, the highest return.

- **Rule 3**—All rates and factors are dependent on the assumptions that were utilized in their calculation.

If an industrial building sold at a seven percent overall rate, which is at the lower end of the range representing lower risk, the estimated or actual rents, vacancy rate, and expenses must also reflect lower risk. If the overall rate indicates low risk, revenue is higher than normal, and vacancy and expenses are lower than normal, and a misleading interpretation of the investment is created. Many investors, loan officers, and developers miss this critical relationship. This brings to mind a cliché—you can't have your cake and eat it too.

- **Rule 4**—The success of all real estate investments is dependent upon the confirmation of all unit indicators.

If a 100,000 square foot office building was purchased for $25,000,000, then the building sold for $250 per square foot. However, if the building was found to be 90,000 square feet, the price per square foot is actually $277.78. Or, if the building was actually 120,000 square feet, it sold for $208.33 per square foot. Because almost all investment decisions and comparisons are made using unit indicators (e.g., price per square foot, price per unit, or price per room), disastrous results occur when a property's physical characteristics (such as lot size, number of units, total square footage, and number of rooms) are not confirmed.

- **Rule 5**—Don't let the numbers override common sense.

If a 5,000 square foot home in a suburban neighborhood is listed at $500 per square foot, or $2,500,000, and all the homes that sold or listed in the past twelve months ranged in price from $1,000,000 to $1,500,000, but had a per square foot ranging from $400 to $550, which data do you believe? Based on the local population's purchasing power, the market for homes in this area can support overall price levels between $1,000,000 to $1,500,000. Additional research will bring to light that that the price per square foot indicators were based on house sizes of 1,818 to 3,750 square feet. Therefore, while factual, the price per square foot indicators were based on very different house sizes. Don't let the numbers mislead you. Always use common sense.

These five helpful economic rules of real estate investment will help solve about ninety percent of the issues encountered when attempting to assess the economics and risk of any real estate investment.

Conclusion: As Simple As That

Over the years, I have been asked thousands questions about real estate investment, including queries about specific property types or locations, where we are in the real estate cycle, or where are capitalization rates. Typically, the final question is simply, "Is this a good deal?" There is never really a finite answer, but there is always a good answer. I can relay it best with the following example:

I was a guest lecturer at the Russian Finance Academy and later bestowed the title of the first American Adjunct Professor. I never spoke a word of Russian to the class, which was attended by a mix of masters and PhD students, professors, and guest attendees from the finance divisions of the government. As I gave lectures on land and rate theories and various investment scenarios, I realized I was not addressing their concern. The blank stares coming from the audience told me that the mysteries they wanted to discover about real estate were not being revealed.

I stood there with my arms folded, looking out over the large auditorium, and realized that as a speaker, a professor (as they called me), and a real estate professional (as I call myself), I had not yet helped solve their problems regarding the when, why, what, where, and how to invest in real estate. Then, I understood. Everything I had learned and was attempting to teach was as simple as the four Russian letters I put on the white board in front of the large crowd:

риск

These four letters were greeted with applause and more focused attention. The four letters revealed to them the context of what I was trying to disclose. Real estate is as simple as that— "Risk". The ability to understand the fundamentals of what creates and enhances value, as well as what defines a project, is all about identifying risk. The problem with most investors, buyers, and sellers is that they forget the fundamentals and get lost in the details or default to ignorance, or worse, arrogance. They forget that the foundation of real estate investing is to comprehend demand, usefulness, scarcity, and money in order to create value, that real estate is enhanced by governmental, economic, social, and environmental factors, and that the project must take into account legal, physical, and financial characteristics in order to achieve the highest value.

Ultimately in that classroom I was able to provide the students with a tool they could use to simply and methodically quantify the overall risk of any real estate investment. I hope this book, which is the direct result of this classroom experience, will do the same for you.